Money is "like" a Bad Dog

Learn how to train your dog, manage your money,
and build financial freedom

The Bellot Family

Money is "like" a Bad Dog

Learn how to train your dog,
manage your money, and build financial freedom

By
The Bellot Family

CONTENTS

Preface

What do managing money and raising a dog have in common?
More than you think.

Why This Title?

The title, *"Money is 'like' a bad dog,"* just like the title of *Marley and Me,* is intentional. This book is a collaborative effort from our family, blending multiple perspectives—just like a conversation around the dinner table. Some people may be accustomed to having this kind of spirited conversation, and the book might flow well for them as they can easily understand multiple perspectives. However, some people who prefer a singular voice may take time to get accustomed to it.

Essentially, we are trying to capture the elephant, much like in *The Blind Men and the Elephant* by John Godfrey Saxe. We knew what "it" was in the end, but getting to "it" revealed different views on what "it" was. Managing money and training a dog seem unrelated—until you realize both require discipline, patience, and consistency. This book will show you how to master both.

A Family Collaboration

I thought about this title as an idea for my sons to write a book. It was a fun way for young people to relate to other young people about financial issues. Another driver for this title was the thought that the young men could use the book as a way to raise money for college. Since then, three of the four young men have been attending college, funded by both cash flow and scholarships.

Since elementary school, they had operated wagon cart stores for some time and did pretty well at it. They have always been entrepreneurial, but with this project, they became curious about budgeting and personal financial management.

How This Book Was Born

When we came up with this idea, we only owned fish as pets. We had several types, including saltwater and freshwater fish. The fish were beautiful, ranging from cichlids to Goby eels. Once set up, the tanks required some maintenance, but they pretty much ran themselves.

For the book, my oldest son came up with some ideas, my second oldest son wrote some down, and my wife and other sons contributed. As stated earlier, an avid reader may notice a variety of writing styles and would be correct because everyone in the family contributed to the writing of this manifesto—or rather, book, blog, or you could even call them notes.

For over 10 years, we contributed and took notes. These notes paid close attention to similarities in how people related to money and dogs, specifically how these traits applied to managing money and achieving various levels of financial freedom.

It was a lot of fun just spending time chatting, laughing, and coming up with crazy analogies. But there was one issue: we never owned a dog. Fish? Check. Speedy the turtle? Check. Batman the robo-parrot? Check. Napoleon the guinea pig? Check. Talk about a snake, rat, or even another turtle after Speedy ran away? All check—but no dog.

I still liked the idea, but we never had a dog.

Finally, after many years, we got a dog—a miniature schnauzer named Sadie.

Learning from Life

Learning isn't exclusive to a classroom or a book. Life presents us with opportunities to make mistakes and learn from our errors, the experiences of others, or our own observations. If we pay enough attention to our experiences, we can improve the ways we gain and apply new information.

We never planned on having a dog, much less using Sadie as the basis for teaching—or being taught—life lessons. But as we moved from owning fish to welcoming Sadie into our family, we realized how much her training mirrored the financial discipline we were striving for.

Managing money, like raising a dog, involves responsibility, planning, and adaptability. Sadie taught us lessons we didn't expect— lessons we are now sharing with you through this book.

Sadie wasn't just a pet—she became our unexpected financial teacher. Here's how she changed everything. We will cover the story of how and why we got Sadie. But first, we want to state for the record that after watching *Marley and Me,* hearing about the reformed Mike Vick, and having our own dog, we do not believe there are bad dogs.

If there are no bad dogs, how does the title even make sense, and how do the analogies work? Just like the story of Sadie, we will get into that too.

The "Money is Like..." Part

Now we get to the first part, the *similitude* part of the title—*"Money is like..."* The whole idea of money management is not a new one, and we do not claim to be experts on money or dogs for that matter.

While our dog is tiny, my aunt raised larger breeds considered aggressive by many. Honestly, while they are beautiful animals, they can be intimidating. I guess that's the same thing with money. We have beautiful dreams of what we would do if we won the Powerball or MegaMillions, but the reality of managing our day-to-day finances can be intimidating.

I don't consider myself or my family to be particularly entertaining or interesting, so while I'd like to spare you the details, they are partially essential to the story. How did we go from being a fish family to owning Sadie?

My sons, like most young people (and older people, for that matter), liked the idea of having things. The issue is that it is easy to say we will act a certain way when we are not actually faced with those situations.

For years, they asked for a dog. They asked for a puppy for Christmas. They asked for a puppy for each of their birthdays—every year. The incessant asking became worse when their godparents got one for Christmas, Shaquille. I became the fascist dictator of parents when I repeatedly said, "No! No dog for you!"

My objections were simple: I did not want a dog, and more importantly, I did not want my wife to take on another responsibility. I reasoned within myself that if we got a dog, Mom (my wife) would be the one taking care of it, performing the duties, and staying on top of everyone else to make sure they did their tasks.

As I kept saying no, I started to realize that my sons were becoming more responsible as they matured. So, my wife and I cleverly came up with a compromise.

The Sadie Compromise

The Sadie compromise was underway! First, they had to perform all of the research about the dog. It had to meet certain criteria:
- Does not shed
- Smart
- Does not bark
- Good family temperament

The second and more important part of the compromise, which our sons were not responsible for, was that we had to be debt-free. We had been listening to the Dave Ramsey show, reading the books recommended by friends, neighbors, and even strangers on planes. Additionally, we were inspired by the debt-free screams from the Dave Ramsey radio show.

While that was a goal, we (I) did not realistically expect to reach this target until all of the boys were out of the house. It turned out we had outsmarted ourselves with the second part of the compromise.

Some may wonder, *why would you place that kind of condition on buying a dog?* We recognized the responsibilities of taking care of a dog. I wanted to ensure that any pet we owned would be cared for without compromising my children's needs.

To our sons' credit, they agreed.

The Journey Ahead

> *"Managing money, like training a dog, requires discipline, adaptability, and patience."*

Before we get to the full story of Sadie, as stated earlier, managing money—like training a dog—requires care, planning and preparation, consistency and routine, patience and perseverance, learning and adapting, and responsibility.
Without the right approach, both can become unruly, but with discipline, they can serve you well.

This book will help you understand personal finance through an unexpected lens: the trials and triumphs of dog training. Each chapter explores relatable stories and actionable tips to help you tame both your dog and your finances.

The Story of Sadie

Early Encounters with Money and Dogs

A s a young person, I had limited experiences with dogs and money. My aunt had three dogs: one that treated me like his natural-born nemesis and constantly jumped on only me, another that acted like my protector, and yet another that guarded the yard but mostly ignored me. I wasn't sure how to feel about dogs because I was nearly bitten by a very well-trained dog that was unfortunately used in dog fights. That dog seemed sad most days, and even when it was sent on the attack and I ran, I never saw it as a bad dog. Instead, I saw it as a sad, handsome, and well-trained creature that would be happier and more beautiful in a different situation.

My first direct encounters with money involved winning some in elementary school academic and artistic contests, losing some in elementary school, and reading enough to build habits and mindsets. Those habits and mindsets followed me into early adulthood and into marriage. My concept of budgeting and debt was simple: keep track of the money that came in via income and keep track of expenses. As long as we could pay our monthly bills, we were good and were not in debt.

Money and dogs were different for Toni. Bear was a dog she grew up with, and the connection was one of affection, not terror. She didn't experience the anxiety of a dog jumping on her exclusively. There were the usual trials and messes that young people either manage or don't manage with dogs, but she had a different experience altogether. Debt held a different weight for her as well. Anytime anyone was owed any amount with payments, she considered it a debt.

The Power of Shared Revelations

After being married and accumulating a number of debts over time—debts for student loans, gym memberships, cars, furniture, credit cards (including candy runs on credit cards), appliances, and even items we don't remember or no longer own—we hit a point of divergence. Toni and I were looking at different pieces of mail that reflected our financial situations.

While I looked at mail showing tiny gains in our bank or investment accounts, she looked at mail reflecting our growing debt. We shared a

10

particularly poignant moment when I eagerly opened bank statements, excitedly noting minuscule gains, while she dejectedly opened bill after bill, revealing our debt. To understand the disparity in our reactions, I added both items together and was astounded to discover that we were indeed in debt, regardless of the definition I chose.

Fortunately for both of us, at the same time we were having this revelation, a neighbor was telling Toni about Dave Ramsey's *Total Money Makeover* and *Financial Peace*. Coincidentally, a very close and dear friend also mentioned those same books to me around that time. Even more surprisingly, while on a business trip, a lady on the plane, out of the blue, mentioned those exact same books as being very good and practical reads. This series of coincidences led us to take action, and we ultimately became debt-free.

How Sadie Changed Everything

What does it mean to be debt-free? It does not mean celebrity wealth or excessive wealth. It does not imply neglecting budgeting, planning, saving, or making sacrifices. However, it did lead us to freedom from "bad" consumer debt, including credit card debt on trivial purchases (like candy bars from 7-11). This experience opened our eyes to a new perspective, one not tied to credit card usage without conscious thought.

We also discovered a supportive community of like-minded individuals through radio and in-person interactions. It was encouraging to hear, see, and know so many other like-minded people.

In sparing the details of the process and noting that this journey is familiar to many, it raises the question: What do these anecdotes have to do with dogs in general and, in particular, Sadie?

Well, you see, one of the agreements we made with the family was that we would not get a dog until we were debt-free! We became a debt-free family many years before we expected, and we finally got a dog. Her name was supposed to be "Ramsey" for obvious reasons, but we named her Sadie because it sounded similar to Mer-'cedes,' and she was better than a Mercedes Benz, which would have been a nice status symbol to acquire after becoming debt-free.

We never expected her to train and delight all of us with the wonderful experiences we encountered from that point on.

Sadie wasn't just a dog; she was a teacher who helped us understand responsibility and preparation in ways we hadn't anticipated when we first considered adding a dog to our family. We underestimated the level of research, effort, and discipline required to care for her. Similarly, when managing finances, many people overlook the need to evaluate their current situation before making decisions.

Much like a pet's unpredictable needs, financial challenges arise unexpectedly, highlighting the importance of preparation. Just as we set criteria for choosing Sadie—non-shedding, smart, and good-tempered—we must also establish clear financial goals that align with our values and capacity. These principles formed the foundation for responsible decisions, ensuring we were ready for both opportunities and challenges.

Takeaway

Before diving into major decisions, whether adopting a pet or creating a financial plan, assess your current circumstances and prepare thoroughly for the first steps to success.

Lessons from Sadie:
- Adapt to unexpected challenges.
- Research thoroughly before making big decisions.
- Embrace collaboration to achieve goals.

Planning and Preparation

Before you can manage your finances—or a dog— you need a solid plan.

The First Steps in Planning

While being a first-time dog owner and managing finances may seem like two completely different things, there are actually some similarities between the two experiences.

When we considered getting a dog, we realized the importance of preparation—from selecting a breed that fit our lifestyle to budgeting for expenses. Every step required planning. Similarly, financial management begins with preparation: setting goals, understanding your resources, and creating a plan that aligns with your priorities. Just as we chose Sadie with care, you must have financial goals that reflect your values and capacity.

We had been coming up with analogy after analogy and having fun doing so. From sleeping on the floor with Sadie on the first night we brought her back from the long road trip, we started to realize we had a lot of planning and preparation to do.

Based on the criteria and research from our sons, the first dog that we looked at was a Giant Schnauzer. He was 8 months old, gorgeous, and, from what we understood, of championship pedigree. From the books and websites we read, this type of dog would not be sold for less than $2,500. Yet the price of this puppy was a very low $500. We were astonished—could it be possible for us to have a Giant Schnauzer for that price?! From the information we had been reading, the Giant would meet all of our criteria.

However, there was one piece of planning and preparation we hadn't accounted for: we had no experience with a real dog—not even dog-sitting or any kind of direct interaction. Additionally, we had not considered the place, space, medical expenses, or transportation needs associated with any dog, much less a dog of this size that required the 'new owner' to be trained as well.

Although the owner was trying to sell the dog, get out of the training business, and move to be closer to his daughter and grandchildren, he fortunately, graciously, and gratefully refused to sell us the dog. We had not done enough planning and preparing.

This lack of preparation is similar to trying to invest for minuscule returns. This happened because we lacked a proper zero-based budget or any real budget structure and assumed everything would work out as long as we were investing. Even if it meant investing $40 a month into eleven different individual stocks while not having an emergency fund?! Yes, it sounds hilarious now, and thank God for good friends who could give you books on budgeting and investing.

Planning to Avoid Surprises

Not planning and not being prepared are the kinds of things that impact you when you bring a puppy home on the first night after a long road trip. This was not like visiting the pet store to purchase pet fish; when you purchase fish, you get everything you need. On the road home with the puppy, however, you realize you don't have any essentials.

Fortunately, there is a pet store on the way home, and you have enough funds to get a few things. You get the puppy home, and the puppy whines and pees inside the house. Because of your limited experience, you may think the puppy is being bad and out of control. Likewise, when you start investing or spending without going through the proper processes, everything looks out of control.

Both raising a puppy and managing finances require a significant amount of planning and preparation. Just as you need to puppy-proof your home and purchase all the necessary supplies before bringing a new puppy home, you also need to create a budget, set financial goals, and research investment options before managing your finances effectively.

On this path, one of the first steps in training a dog—and in training your money—is choosing a name. If you don't name the dog and train it to respond to its name, it will be motivated by its animal instincts and may even try to lead the pack. Likewise, if you don't give every dollar you earn a name, you end up chasing after it and serving it.

What's in a Name?

As part of planning and preparing for a puppy, choosing a name enhances the bond and plays a role in the training process. Teaching a dog its name involves an exchange of your attention and treats for the dog's attention and compliance. The name is an important part of planning and preparing, just like deciding what language you are going to speak to the dog in.

This leads to a consistent approach in positive reinforcement, which has proven to be an effective training technique applicable to various types of training. The language can be English, Spanish, German, Elvish, Klingon—anything, really. There just has to be a consistent plan for the language you choose.

Likewise, you have to plan ahead for how rewards will be given and administered. Rewarding desired behaviors with treats, praise, or playtime will obviously encourage the dog to repeat those behaviors. This approach is seen as more effective and humane than using punishment or negative reinforcement, like the old newspaper-on-the-nose techniques.

By implementing these strategies, you will pave the way for your named dog to respond to you and become a member of your pack.

Planning for money is similar, but the major difference is that the realities of life typically arrive before you've named your money, established a language, or set up a plan of rewards. Naming your money is important so that you and it respond appropriately to each other.

It's often said that people will do all sorts of things for money, but if you name money a servant, a tool, or even an inanimate object, you'll be compelled to examine your own motives. You wouldn't call money a hero you expect to save the day.

As part of the plan and preparation, once money has a name, the next step is the language you use to talk about it. That language might include phrases like:

- "You will help me take care of my affairs."
- "You will help me take care of my family."
- "You will help me take care of others."
- "You will work in the best way possible to grow and multiply even when I'm not working."
- "You will follow after the things I follow and value."

With this language in place, you can plan the proper times, places, and types of rewards that should be in place beyond responding to purely emotional situations.

The Importance of Preparation

The joy of owning a dog or achieving financial freedom is rooted in preparation. Before bringing Sadie home, we learned the hard way that having the right supplies, space, and knowledge makes all the difference. Likewise, financial planning requires careful preparation, setting budgets, creating an emergency fund, and researching investment opportunities.

When we almost brought home a Giant Schnauzer without considering our limitations, it mirrored how some people dive into investments without understanding the risks. The lesson was clear: planning prevents being overwhelmed and avoids unnecessary failures. Just as we adjusted our plans for Sadie, you can create a financial roadmap that aligns with your needs and resources.

Takeaway

Prepare for success by planning ahead. Whether it's a dog or your finances, research, set realistic goals, and establish safeguards to avoid unnecessary stress and missteps.

Planning for a Dog	Planning Your Finances
Research breeds	Research budgeting methods
Estimate costs for food/vet	Calculate monthly expenses
Buy Supplies (leash, toys)	Open required accounts

How to get started with finances:
- Write down all monthly expenses.
- Define your financial goals.
- Create a budget based on reality.
- Write the plan for where you want to go.

Consistency and Routine

What Sadie Taught Us About Consistency

Consistency and routine are important aspects of both raising a puppy and managing finances. When we got Sadie, and as new dog owners, this was something we had not thought about. For example, some of us burn the candle at both ends, while others prefer a full, prescribed 8 hours of sleep. How did this impact Sadie? She did not know if she was coming or going!

Was she going to eat when she first got up and then go outside? Or was she going to eat when *whoever* got up and stay inside for a half-hour? Was it okay to chew the squeaky toy at 10:30 pm, and were Jabra headphones part of her chew toy package? We didn't consider how a lack of consistency and routine would impact this new endeavor.

We soon realized that establishing a consistent sleeping, feeding, exercise, and play schedule was crucial to Sadie's health and well-being, just as establishing a consistent savings plan or budget is crucial to financial stability.

Sadie's first few weeks with us were not as smooth as we would have hoped, and to be honest, we're not sure they could have gone any better. At first, we didn't stick to a routine for Sadie, and she struggled. The same happens with money—without consistency, finances spiral out of control.

Without a clear feeding or exercise schedule, Sadie seemed confused and in an unstable environment. We quickly learned that consistency, whether in her training or our finances, is the key to success. Establishing routines such as regular budget reviews or consistent saving plans builds stability and trust. Just as Sadie thrived with clear expectations, your financials will flourish with disciplined routines.

Building a routine for Long-term success

The first part of consistency and routine is recognizing the importance and necessity of care and attention. Additionally, in this chapter, we will use a few puppy stories, so here is the gratuitous disclaimer:

So, let's begin with some facts that people who grew up with dogs already know, and that new dog owners soon discover: Dogs get matted, constipated, their teeth go bad, and their mental health is affected without daily care and scheduled poop scoops.

Before getting a dog, it is worth paying attention to the care and attention required in taking care of a dog. They need grooming, they need to be brushed, and you have to watch what they eat—their diet (everything that goes into their mouths), their teeth, playtime, exercise (as opposed to play, this is structured physical activity), and socialization.

Yes, their daily care and mental well-being are affected if this care and attention are not given consistently. With financial management, including investing, it is important to build a routine where you consistently look at everything.

Whether you think you have a little or a lot, you need to look at what you spend on, the bills that come in (including subscriptions), the bank accounts, and any savings or investment accounts. Just like dogs, investing and saving money need "some" care and attention. Fortunately, it's not like walking around with a pooper scooper, but it's not too far from it.

When we are consistent in our routine, we have a scenario of:

Little Dog Bark at the Big Dog Behind the Fence

We teach the puppy that it is part of the pack and is working for the good of the house while enjoying the perks. Our money behaves in a "similar" manner, where small efforts have the beginnings of a much larger impact.

Have you heard of followers? In our modern world, social media followers are quite common. Interestingly, this concept has become a way for social media platforms and "influencers" to generate revenue. Now, let's talk about the dog world.

Just like in social media, dogs have a natural hierarchy. The weakest dogs are at the bottom, while the strongest and most dominant dogs are at the top. Everyone else in the pack follows the leader. So, how does this relate to money being like a "bad" dog?

Well, when you get a new puppy, you need to establish a consistent routine to show it that you're the boss of the house (leader of the pack). Similarly, when you earn money from your hard work, you need to make sure that money goes where you want it to go. This happens by establishing consistency and routine.

> *Try this:* Write down one daily habit that helps your finances, like checking your budget or transferring money to savings. Just like a dog's routine, your financial habits should be predictable and consistent.

Consistency and routine are key when it comes to raising a puppy and managing your finances. By sticking to regular feeding and sleep schedules for your furry friend, or maintaining a consistent spending and savings plan, you create stability in both areas and keep everything in order.

Discipline is the Key: I Lead, and She Follows!

I'm not sure where I'm headed, so the puppy and the money go where they please.

Many of us like the idea of being in charge, but beneath the surface, we often feel uneasy and uncertain. It seems effortless when we have to give someone specific instructions, but deep down, we have mixed feelings.

We enjoy telling people what to do, but we're also uncomfortable doing so. Having a dog reflects this dichotomy, and these questions become evident in the dog's behavior because, truth be told, sometimes we argue with ourselves.

We wonder if we're too lenient or too strict and what people will think. (We're surrounded by dog lovers and those who don't have dogs but have opinions.) These questions linger in our minds: Should my puppy sleep in my bed or in a crate? Should I let it on my couch or not? Should it be a family member or just a pet?

On the financial front, we face dilemmas: Should I adopt a zero-based budgeting approach, traditional accounting/budgeting, or should I ignore it and worry about it later when the bills come in? Should I buy new clothes or use what I already have?

All of these questions are on my mind when thinking about these types of things. But whatever I do, it will require consistency in my routine. The path not taken will make a puppy and money seem out of control when I flip-flop and remain inconsistent in my routine.

Playtime

One area where you can be consistent and establish a routine with your puppy is through playtime. We often see people having fun with their dogs playing frisbee or fetch on television. This should have been one of the things we researched when looking into dogs and different breeds, or maybe not, as we would have missed out on the special joys of Sadie.

Fortunately, we didn't call her a 'bad dog' when she enjoyed playing the way she did.

Learning to play fetch with your puppy and your finances is an engaging metaphor for real investing, not just throwing money at anything and hoping for the best. In the game of fetch, some puppies naturally excel at playing fetch, while others don't.

The objective is to throw an object, and the dog retrieves and returns it. However, as many dog owners know, this doesn't always happen. Sadie wasn't a very good fetch dog, which is unfortunate because it is more likely her owners weren't good fetch trainers either.

She would bring you a ball, and you'd get excited, thinking, *"Oh wow! She wants to play fetch!"* But it seemed like she was saying, *"Please throw this ball where you want me to lay and chew it, preferably in the shade."*

Some of you may relate to that.

Investing is like playing fetch—when done right, you send your money out and expect it to return with gains. But, like Sadie, sometimes your investments don't come back the way you planned. You want to send your money out in different vehicles, and you want it to return to you in the form of dividends, returns, interest, and the like.

Just a heads-up—just as Sadie didn't always bring the ball back the way we wanted, some returns may not come back right away.

However, just as she continued to play, you can expect returns over time.

To repeat, when you save and invest money, you expect it to come back in the form of dividends, returns, and interest—though not always immediately.

This chapter emphasizes the need for strategic planning and awareness in investing, ensuring that your financial efforts yield returns over time, much like a successful game of fetch rather than a casual throw into the unknown.

Keep Going—Right now, discipline might feel like a drag, but it's actually a shortcut to peace. Keep going, and you'll see the rewards!

When we are consistent in our routine, we have a scenario of the little dog barking at the big dog behind the fence. Most people, even the most devoted dog lovers, can picture the "little yappy, happy puppy…" barking at the big dog.

Well, we teach the puppy that he is part of the pack, that he is working for the good of the house, and that he enjoys the perks. Our money behaves in a *similar* manner, where small amounts are the beginnings of a much larger impact. However, it does start making 'noise' and burning a hole in your pocket, tempting you to look at bigger financial commitments before it's time.

Grandma said, *"Every time you get some money, save $5."* You get the picture…

The Story of Buddy

Imagine a small dog named Buddy, a friendly and curious pup living in a cozy house in a quiet neighborhood. Despite his petite size, Buddy had a big bark and was known for his protective nature toward his home.

One sunny day, while playing in his yard, Buddy spotted a large dog named Roxie walking by on the other side of the fence. Roxie was a beautiful Saint Bernard with fluffy fur and a friendly demeanor. However, Buddy initially mistook her for a strange, big dog intruding on his territory.

Buddy immediately started barking, trying to scare Roxie away. But Roxie remained calm and patient, understanding Buddy's protective instincts. Despite Buddy's continued yipping, barking, and growling,

Roxie patiently waited for Buddy's owner to arrive and resolve the situation.

When Buddy's owner came out, he smiled and greeted Roxie, allowing Buddy to meet her properly. Buddy's owner knew that despite his intimidating bark, Buddy was actually a gentle soul. Buddy watched as his owner warmly welcomed Roxie and offered her a treat. Still cautious, Buddy sniffed Roxie's scent through the fence. However, when Roxie approached him slowly and gently licked his nose, Buddy's tail began to wag tentatively.

Though they were cordial, they were not yet truly friendly. Buddy still yipped a lot, and Roxie preferred a quieter, more peaceful environment. Some days, Roxie grumbled about the noise. Inside her doghouse, she muttered, *"That infernal yipping! Can't a dog get some peace?"* She peeked out of the doghouse door, squinting at the source of the commotion.

Across the yard, bounding and barking with boundless joy and an eye toward protection, was Buddy, the tiny puppy. He was a whirlwind of energy—a tiny tornado of fur and yaps. He chased his own tail, barked at butterflies, and yipped with delight at the slightest breeze while keeping an eye on the fence to protect his home.

Roxie, a seasoned veteran of neighborhood "bark-offs," scoffed at Buddy's antics.

"What a ridiculous creature. All bark and no bite," she thought, retreating further into her doghouse, grumbling about the disturbance.

But Buddy, oblivious to Roxie's disdain, continued his energetic frolics.

Then, he spotted a particularly enticing stick and joyfully launched himself after it. The stick was larger than he had anticipated, and despite his valiant efforts, Buddy was swept off his feet, tumbling head over heels and landing in a heap of soft dirt.

Roxie, despite her initial annoyance, couldn't help but snicker. She poked her head out of the doghouse. *"Need a hand, pup?"*

Buddy, bewildered and slightly embarrassed, looked up at the larger dog and whimpered. To her surprise, Roxie found herself amused. She cautiously approached Buddy, nudging the stick with her nose. *"Here, let's get you back on your feet."*

With a gentle nudge, Roxie helped Buddy to his paws. Buddy, shaken but unharmed, wagged his tail furiously in gratitude and licked Roxie's nose, a gesture of canine affection.

Buddy and Roxie became the best of friends. They'd meet at the fence, wagging their tails and sharing treats. Buddy was always on guard for his home, while Roxie respected his space and never crossed the fence. Even when a strange dog tried to sneak into Buddy's yard, Buddy barked so loudly that he scared the intruder away. Buddy's owner was so proud of him that he gave him a special treat.

Buddy and Roxie, despite their differences, learned valuable lessons from each other. Buddy taught Roxie to appreciate the simple joys of life, such as the warmth of the sun, the exhilaration of a good chase, and the sheer delight of a new scent. In return, Roxie imparted the importance of caution and patience and the wisdom of choosing battles wisely.

Ultimately, Buddy and Roxie demonstrated that even the smallest dogs can be formidable protectors of their homes and families. Their friendship blossomed in an unexpected place, proving that true character lies beyond outward appearances and that life is full of unexpected connections.

Some Lessons from the Puppy and Finances

- **Appearances can be deceiving.**
    - o Roxie initially judged Buddy based on his size and boisterous behavior. She learned that true character goes beyond outward appearances.
    - o Likewise, putting aside $5 whenever you get some money, even when it doesn't seem like much, allows you to develop the discipline learned from this process.
    - o It may seem like budgeting makes you look poor or like you don't have money, but the irony is that ALL of the largest companies in the world operate off of budgets.

- **Life is full of unexpected connections.**
    - o Roxie and Buddy, two dogs with vastly different personalities, formed a strong bond, demonstrating that unlikely friendships can be the most rewarding.
    - o We all know how to count, and to use an example from Grandma: You can never count to $1,000 if you don't first count $5. Unexpected connections often come from small beginnings. Recognizing how small habits impact larger decisions is key to financial success.

- **Overcoming differences.**
    - o Their friendship thrived because they learned to embrace their differences and appreciate what they could learn from each other.
    - o There are many differing views on money and personal finance, but by identifying common principles, we can find a path to financial success.

In the end, Buddy's small size and big bark proved to be a powerful combination. He showed that even the smallest dogs can be fierce protectors of their homes and families.

Buddy, a small but protective dog, initially clashed with Roxie, a larger dog, but they eventually became friends. Good habits with small things align very nicely with foundational habits for big things. Through consistency and routine, even in small beginnings, their friendship teaches valuable lessons about appearances, unexpected connections, and overcoming differences—lessons that impact our consistency and routine in life.

This also applies to finances. Buddy's owner was rewarded by the discipline he developed, as well as the protective nature and knowledge gained from starting small. Similarly, Buddy learned that he was part of a pack.

Find a Key in the Routine

Consistency and routine are key in both personal finance and dog training. Tracking expenses and using consistent commands—along with regular practice and immediate rewards—lead to desired outcomes in both areas. Adapting routines and staying informed are also important for long-term success.

Consistency transformed Sadie from a misguided and misled puppy into a disciplined companion. Establishing routines like regular feeding, exercise, and training sessions created a sense of stability and trust. In personal finance, similar routines—such as budgeting, tracking expenses, and automating savings—are essential for long-term success.

Establishing a consistent schedule for a puppy, including feeding, exercise, and playtime, is vital for their health and well-being, just as maintaining a consistent savings plan or budget is crucial for financial stability. Discipline and routine help build stability and trust, whether for a puppy or for finances, leading to better outcomes.

Investing, like playing fetch with a puppy, requires strategic planning and patience for long-term returns. Buddy and Roxie's friendship illustrates that appearances can be deceiving, unexpected connections can be rewarding, and differences can be overcome. Small financial habits, like saving $5, can lead to significant results over time.

Different views on money and personal finances exist, but common denominators can guide us. Buddy, a small dog, demonstrates that even small beginnings can lead to significant rewards through discipline and consistency.

For instance, just as Sadie learned to associate her name with rewards and purpose, you can name every dollar in your budget to give it a purpose. As an example, sticking to a rule like the 50/30/20 rule can help your money work for you, not against you. And guess what? Routine can also help you stay disciplined, whether it's with your furry friends or your finances.

Rule	Description
• 50% for needs	• Mortgage, rent, utilities, etc.
• 30% for wants	• Clothing, entertainment, etc.
• 20% for savings and giving	• Retirement

Takeaway

Consistency isn't restrictive—it's empowering. Routine builds trust, structure, and progress, both in dog training and in managing your personal financial health.

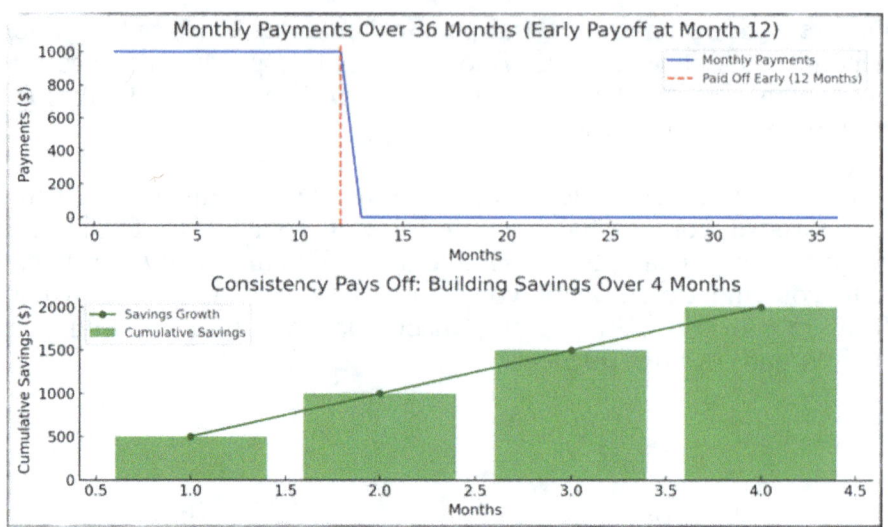

- These two graphs show how consistency pays off:
  - Professional investors state that you cannot guarantee returns. The first graph shows that you can achieve a 100% return on your $1,000 in month 13 if you pay off a bill early.
  - The second graph is a visual timeline showing how $500 saved over four months can accumulate and be used for an emergency fund or another financial goal.

Patience and Perseverance

Is That a Rabbit?

Money, like a dog, is in some respects an excellent servant but a terrible master. One has to understand the importance of managing money carefully. Just like a dog, money can be a useful tool when controlled properly, but it can also become destructive when not managed carefully.

Both raising a puppy and managing finances require patience and perseverance. Puppies can be challenging to train, and it takes time and effort to establish good financial habits and reach your financial goals. Just like an untrained dog dashes after distractions, money can slip away if you're not in control. "Rabbit Syndrome" describes impulsive spending habits that derail financial goals.

Training Sadie required patience, especially when she exhibited what we have come to call "Rabbit Syndrome"—darting off impulsively at every distraction. Managing money often feels the same, with temptations like impulse purchases or high-risk investments pulling you off course. Patience and perseverance mean staying focused on your long-term goals, even when progress feels slow. The discipline to stay the course, much like reining in a distracted dog, yields lasting rewards.

> Sadie's Rabbit Syndrome
> Sadie couldn't resist chasing after every distraction. Managing money is no different—without focus, it's easy to lose control.

Patience and perseverance mean knowing that you don't have everything figured out yet. Specifically, patience is the capacity to endure waiting, delay, or provocation without becoming annoyed or angry, and perseverance is steadfastness in effort despite difficulty or delay. Both are essential for success in both puppy training and personal finance.

In puppy training, patience is vital for understanding the puppy's learning pace and handling setbacks calmly. Perseverance is required for consistent effort, overcoming challenges, and maintaining long-term commitment. Similarly, in personal finance, patience is crucial for reaching financial goals, weathering market fluctuations, and paying off debt. Perseverance is needed to stick to a budget, resist impulse purchases, and recover from financial setbacks.

Both endeavors demand consistent effort, the ability to learn from mistakes, and a positive approach despite challenges. No matter what, you'll keep moving forward—one step at a time—until you've built the foundational pieces and the necessary building blocks. That way, you'll be ready to bring this puppy home and have your finances in a better place.

The Importance of Control: A Lesson from Chippy

In our community, we have a *leash law*. This means that dogs must be leashed when in public.

So, imagine our surprise as we were driving home through a very busy intersection and saw a woman in the middle of the road, desperately trying to catch her loose dog while avoiding an unfortunate, messy accident. *"Come here, Chippy!!"* she cried, but the dog was always one step ahead of her. It looked like an accident waiting to happen, but we had to leave before we saw how it ended.

Later, we checked the news reports and didn't see any accidents at that major intersection, so we were relieved that nothing had happened to Chippy. But this incident started a conversation about Sadie's interactions with the neighborhood rabbits and squirrels.

In her case, it seemed like she didn't want them on her lawn. *"Get off my lawn!"* she would bark. However, when on walks in the open— just 10 to 20 feet away from rabbits—she tended to mind her own business.

That was great—she was a **lady!**

It took patience and perseverance to get her to that point—to walk like a lady on her walks. Yes, she still liked to sniff around, but as long as nothing was immediately in front of her, she didn't care what the rabbits did or which dog barked from their house.

This taught us important lessons about patience and perseverance, which we will explore next—because **Sadie was not the only dog we took on that walk to the park. Oh no!**

To protect the innocent, we will not disclose the dog's name, but the difference between that dog and Sadie taught us about Rabbit Syndrome.

Just like Chippy almost caused a disaster, this particular dog ran into the street after a rabbit, narrowly avoiding being hit by cars. The chaos that followed was remarkable—multiple people jumped out of their vehicles to try to help, the dog zigzagged across both sides of the street, neighbors rushed out of their homes with doors left wide open, and even other dogs ran out, joining in the commotion to assist in bringing the runaway dog back to its frazzled owner.

In the context of money being "like" a bad dog, Rabbit Syndrome can be likened to a dog that takes off running when startled, such as when someone shouts, *"Rabbit!"* or *"Squirrel!"* Similarly, without proper training, money can escape from your grasp, be mismanaged, and quickly disappear.

The Rabbit Syndrome Chronicles

In the world of personal finance, navigating the unpredictable terrain can be akin to handling a dog caught in the grip of Rabbit Syndrome.

Imagine this: Fido, your four-legged companion, suddenly darts away as if a thunderous call of *"Rabbit!"* has echoed through the air. The chase is on, and Fido's instincts take over, heedless of the potential dangers ahead.

Much like Fido's impulsive sprint, our relationship with money often mirrors this unpredictable dash. Without proper financial training, we find ourselves chasing after opportunities without a clear plan, reacting to every financial impulse as if someone just shouted, *"Squirrel!"* We pursue the elusive idea of wealth without a leash, allowing our financial instincts to dictate our actions.

Just as Fido requires training to effectively channel his energy and instincts, so does our approach to money. Without financial education and discipline, we risk chasing every fleeting opportunity, only to realize the pursuit has led us astray. The elusive "rabbit" may represent various financial temptations—quick gains, speculative investments, or even the pressure of keeping up with others.

Consider this: With proper training, Fido can be guided, redirected, and taught to distinguish between genuine opportunities and fleeting distractions. Similarly, by cultivating financial literacy and discipline, we can bring order to the chaos of our financial pursuits. The pursuit of wealth should be a deliberate, strategic journey rather than a frenzied chase after every passing "rabbit."

Try This: Actionable Strategies to Combat Impulse Spending
- Create a "Financial Leash" checklist with rules like:
  - Wait 24 hours before making a purchase over an agreed amount ($100 for some, more for others).
  - Use cash instead of credit for non-essential expenses.
  - Set a monthly "fun spending" limit to avoid overspending.

It's not easy or fast, but just as a well-trained dog responds to commands, our financial education becomes the leash that guides our money's path. Understanding the nuances of investments, budgeting, and long-term planning serves as obedience training for our financial future. With a trained financial mindset, we can confidently navigate the twists and turns of the economic landscape, avoiding the pitfalls that often trip up the unprepared.

In the end, Rabbit Syndrome teaches us a valuable lesson: It's not the existence of rabbits or squirrels that poses the real problem—it's our response to them.

Likewise, in the realm of money, it's not the presence of opportunities or challenges that determines success but rather the quality of our financial training that shapes our journey.

So, let's embark on the training grounds, leashes in hand, ready to guide our financial future through the unpredictable but rewarding adventure of wealth-building.

Getting a Few Things Under Control

There are tools that can help control Rabbit Syndrome with patience and perseverance.

Personal finance and training share many similarities. Just like in any type of training, setting clear and measurable goals is critical in personal finance. Financial well-being requires discipline and consistent effort. This means sticking to a budget, saving money, and avoiding unnecessary expenses.

Personal finance also requires continuous education and learning. Just like dog training, you must keep up with the latest financial news, understand investment options, and stay informed about money management strategies. Developing good financial habits and sticking to them requires regular tracking of expenses, reviewing budgets, and making informed financial decisions.

Economic conditions, income levels, and financial goals change over time, so you must be flexible and adjust your financial plans accordingly.

Best Practices for Personal Finance

Budgeting

The primary apprehension associated with budgeting, financial planning, or spending plans is the fear of confronting aspects of life that feel out of control. However, it is crucial to recognize that a budget is not inherently positive or negative—instead, your perspective on budgeting may need a shift.

Just as learning to give commands to a puppy involves establishing who is in charge and who should follow, budgeting involves creating a structured plan for managing income and expenses.

To achieve this:
- Track your income and expenses to gain a clear understanding of your financial situation.
- Prioritize financial objectives and allocate funds accordingly.
- Regularly review and update your budget to reflect any changes in circumstances.

Saving and Investing

- Build an emergency fund to cover unexpected expenses.
- For some, saving $1,000 for immediate emergencies may seem simple, while for others, it may feel overwhelming.
- The difference between getting a tow for a flat tire or leaving your car on the side of the road for a week often depends on whether you have an emergency fund.
- Try to save a percentage of your income regularly toward your emergency fund goals.

Managing Debt

- Pay off credit cards and loans to reduce high-interest debt.
- Use the snowball method (pay off smaller debts first) or the avalanche method (pay off high-interest debts first).
- If needed, consolidate debt or negotiate with creditors to lower interest rates or payment terms.

Planning for Retirement

- If you're young, you may say, "I have plenty of time." If you're older, you may think, "That time has passed me by."
- The crucial thing is to take action and remain engaged in financial planning, regardless of market conditions.
- Contribute to retirement accounts like 401(k)s or IRAs and take advantage of employer matching programs.
- Regularly review and adjust your retirement savings based on your financial goals and risk tolerance.

Insurance and Protection

- Ensure you have adequate insurance coverage, including health, life, and property insurance, to protect against unexpected events.

- Review your insurance policies periodically to ensure they still meet your needs.
- Consider long-term care insurance to prepare for potential healthcare expenses in old age.

Continuous Learning

- Stay updated on financial news, trends, and investment options.
- Read books, attend seminars, or take courses to improve financial literacy.
- Seek guidance from financial professionals if needed.

Additional Personal Finance Tips

- Clearly differentiate between needs and wants and make conscious spending decisions.
- Focus on building wealth over material possessions.
- Avoid relying on credit cards for everyday expenses—this is one habit that will always have you chasing the *Rabbit!*
- Set up automatic savings and bill payments to stay on track.
- Review and eliminate unnecessary subscriptions or recurring expenses.
- Negotiate better deals on insurance premiums, utility bills, and other services.
- Wait before making non-essential purchases to avoid impulse spending.
- Take advantage of tax-saving strategies such as contributing to retirement accounts or using deductions.
- Teach your children about personal finance from an early age to help them develop smart money habits.
- Find an accountability partner, such as a support group or financial mentor, to stay motivated and on track.

"Remember, personal finance is a journey, and achieving financial well-being requires discipline, continuous learning, and adaptability."

Training Your Furry Friend: Best Practices for Dog Training

If you don't have a puppy or plan on getting one, hang in there with us—it all connects. If you are an experienced dog owner, this might seem elementary, but we tried to cover something for everyone.

Just like with managing finances, patience and perseverance are essential when training a dog. Dogs thrive on routine and understand what's expected of them when they receive consistent cues and follow the same commands.

It's especially important to establish a system of rewards, consequences, and consistency. Dogs learn best through repetition, so make sure to use clear and predictable commands to avoid confusion.

Positive Reinforcement in Dog Training

- Positive reinforcement is a fantastic training method that works wonders for dogs and other animals.
- Rewarding good behaviors with treats, praise, or playtime encourages dogs to repeat those behaviors.
- This approach is much more effective and humane than punishment or negative reinforcement.
- Dogs, like people, are motivated by rewards, so positive reinforcement helps them associate good behaviors with positive outcomes.

Clear Communication is Key

- Dogs don't understand human language, so it's important to use clear and consistent cues.
- Training commands should be short, simple, and easily distinguishable.
- Consistency in body language and tone of voice also helps dogs understand what's expected of them.
- Clear communication builds a strong bond between you and your dog.

Patience and Persistence in Dog Training

- Dogs may not grasp commands or behaviors immediately, and it can take time for them to learn and retain information.
- Patience and persistence allow the dog to learn at their own pace and gradually improve their skills.
- Training a dog is a rewarding experience that requires patience, consistency, and positive reinforcement.

Helpful Dog Training Tips

Start Early and Be Proactive

- Puppies have a critical learning period between 3-14 weeks of age.
- Teaching basic commands like sit, stay, and come early helps your dog become a well-behaved member of the family.
- Being proactive in training prevents unwanted behaviors and shapes good habits.

Use Positive Reinforcement

- Positive reinforcement strengthens the bond between you and your dog.
- Rewarding desired behaviors with treats, praise, or playtime encourages good habits.
- This approach makes training a positive experience for both of you.

Keep Training Sessions Short and Frequent

- Dogs have short attention spans, so training sessions should be brief and focused (10-15 minutes).
- Frequent training sessions help reinforce learned behaviors.
- Spacing out sessions throughout the day allows dogs to process and retain information better.

Be Consistent with Rules and Boundaries

- Consistency is key in training.
- Establish clear rules and boundaries so your dog knows what's expected.
- Everyone in the household should follow the same rules to avoid confusion.

Use Appropriate Training Aids

- Training aids like clickers, treats, and toys can help reinforce good behavior.
- But be mindful—dogs should not become overly dependent on training aids.

Training a dog is a gradual process that requires patience, consistency, and positive reinforcement.
- A clicker acts as a "magic wand" that tells your dog, *"Hey, you did that right!"*
- Treats are small rewards for good behavior.
- Toys keep your dog engaged and motivated during training.

If you're struggling with training or dealing with behavioral issues, don't hesitate to ask for help from a certified dog trainer or behaviorist.

In Short, training a dog is like training your finances:
- Consistency, positive reinforcement, clear communication, patience, and persistence are key.
- Early training, positive reinforcement, and short, frequent sessions lead to long-term success.
- Following rules, using appropriate training aids, and seeking professional help when needed can make all the difference.

The Connection Between Dogs and Money

Both training a dog and managing finances require discipline, adaptability, and long-term thinking. By applying these principles, you can train your financial habits just as effectively as you train a well-behaved dog.

Let discipline and consistency lead the way!

Stay Focused on the Long Game

Money, like a dog, can be a valuable tool when managed properly but can become destructive without control. You can encounter "Rabbit Syndrome," which, if left unchecked, can be harmful.

"Rabbit Syndrome" in the context of money refers to impulsive and uncontrolled financial behavior, akin to a dog chasing after distractions without a leash. Both raising a puppy and managing finances require patience and perseverance, as they involve consistent effort, learning from mistakes, and maintaining a positive approach despite challenges.

Training Sadie required patience, especially when she had Rabbit Syndrome or other setbacks. Similarly, building financial security is not a quick process. It takes time to pay off debt, build an emergency fund, or see returns on investments. Yet perseverance in the face of challenges yields lasting rewards.

In both cases, setbacks are learning opportunities. When Sadie didn't grasp a command right away, we adjusted our approach. Likewise, if a financial goal seems out of reach, reassess your strategy without losing sight of the bigger picture. Progress may be slow, but it's steady and meaningful.

Takeaway

Here are a few distractions that require patience and perseverance to overcome:

Financial Distractions	Pet Distractions
Impulse Buying – Purchasing items on a whim, falling for sales, and unnecessary spending.	**Rabbit Syndrome** – Chasing after rabbits, squirrels, and impulses without thinking.
Retail Therapy – Using shopping to cope with emotions instead of mindful spending.	**Destructive Chewing** – Pets chewing on furniture and household items when left unchecked.
Keeping Up with the Joneses – Spending to maintain appearances with neighbors, peers, or social media.	**Excessive Barking** – Barking uncontrollably at strangers, other animals, or noises.

Patience and perseverance aren't just "nice-to-have" traits—they are the keys to building a strong financial future.

Success requires, in addition to patience, resilience and embracing challenges as part of the journey. Moving forward, small steps are essential to achieving significant outcomes.

Learning and Adapting

We Didn't Know

D on't expect "it" to be quick—expect it to be a lot, and don't be overwhelmed.

As a first-time dog owner and a novice in actively managing finances, there is a lot to learn. You will need to educate yourself on proper dog care and training techniques, just as you will need to educate yourself on personal finance concepts and investment strategies. Moreover, both require adaptation to new situations and unforeseen circumstances.

> *"One day, as we watched Sadie sniff around the backyard, it dawned on us how much her behavior mirrored our financial habits..."*

When we got Sadie, everyone said they were all in on taking care of her and training her. But that learning experience didn't happen as planned.

In early fall, we often spotted mice in the backyard. You'd think a dog of Sadie's size would love the chance to bark and chase mice, but this became our second learning experience.

Sadie was as afraid of mice as many humans. She would see a mouse in the corner or hear it rustling under the leaves and immediately stand behind us, looking up as if to say, *"Aren't you going to do something about that?!"*

As afraid as she was of mice at first, she eventually learned and adapted. She got to the point where, if you were outside and pointed to an area saying *"Sadie, mouse"*, she would rush over, sniffing the area, searching for a mouse. She cornered and trapped several field mice in the backyard. If you didn't give her a specific location, she would patrol the fence and corners of the yard, sniffing for intruders.

We learned alongside her, adapting to the mouse situation.

Learning from Small Habits

Another lesson: dogs poop all over the yard. Lesson number three? Not Sadie.

She had one specific spot in the backyard—*her spot*. If you took her outside and she needed to relieve herself, she would go to *her* designated area.

This was great! Only one area to clean up. And oh, how she loved when it was cleaned and sprayed down. She would run back and forth across the yard as if she had been given a new toy or a treat.

When Sadie Got Sick—Another Lesson in Adapting

The first time Sadie got sick challenged everything we thought we had learned.

Sadie got constipated and then had diarrhea. We had not yet learned about the magic of pumpkins.

We *expected* everyone in the house to help watch her throughout the evening.

But nooooooo — 'everyone' went to sleep, and only two people stayed up with her as she whimpered in discomfort.

During that long night, she asked to go out frequently and urgently. She would try to run to her *spot*, but halfway there, she wouldn't make it.

You remember how afraid she was of mice? She would run back into the house and look up at us in the same manner—helpless and seeking guidance.

Staying up all night with her made going to school and work really tough the next day for a couple of people.

But we learned and adapted. We realized:
1. Dogs get sick.
2. We didn't have all the necessary tools and knowledge at the time.
3. Next time, we would be better prepared.

And guess what? Sadie learned, too. She became more confident in our ability to take care of her.

What We Learned from Sadie's Fear of Mice

- Flexibility helps you overcome challenges.
- Seek help and education when facing new obstacles.
- Preparation prevents stress in tough times.

Sadie was afraid of mice when we first brought her home, but over time, she adapted and became a fearless hunter.

This taught us a valuable lesson about flexibility. In financial management, adapting to unexpected challenges—like a market downturn or sudden expense—is crucial.

Just as Sadie learned to confront her fears, you can build resilience by continuously learning and refining your approach to finances.

This includes:
- Acknowledging what you don't know.
- Finding people who can help you learn.
- Understanding that mistakes happen—but you adapt and move forward.

The Trainers Story

The dog trainer is a young man who loves dogs and wants to make a living by training them. He has learned some basic skills from his father, who was also a dog trainer, but he wants to improve his knowledge and income. He hears about a famous dog trainer named BethMari, who lives in Brush and is known as the richest woman in the city. He decides to travel to Brush and seek her advice.

The dog trainer sets off on his journey with his loyal dog, Rex. Along the way, he meets various people who offer him different advice on how to become rich and successful. Some tell him to gamble—he could play Powerball, MegaMillions, or any of the gambling apps. Some tell him to borrow money, including using margin trading and investing in 'meme' crypto and stocks. Others encourage him to invest in risky ventures.

He also encounters many dangers and challenges—bandits, wild animals, and harsh weather. He tries some of the advice he receives, but none of it works for him. He loses money, gets into debt, and faces trouble.

Finally, the dog trainer arrives in Brush and finds BethMari's place. He is amazed by the wealth and luxury he sees there. He requests an audience with BethMari and is granted one after waiting several days. He tells BethMari his story and asks her for her secrets to success.

BethMari listens patiently and then tells him that she will teach him seven principles of financial wisdom, which she learned from an old sage named Mr. Solomon when she was young.

BethMari explains each principle to the dog trainer, using examples from her own life and from ancient history. The principles are:
- *Pay yourself first*: Save at least 10% of your income before spending on anything else.
- *Control your expenses*: Live within your means and avoid unnecessary luxuries.
- *Make your money work for you*: Invest your savings wisely in profitable ventures that offer security and good returns.
- *Protect your wealth*: Avoid losses by being cautious and staying away from scams.
- *Increase your earning ability*: Learn new skills, seek opportunities, and work hard to improve your value.
- *Insure your future*: Plan ahead for emergencies, retirement, and legacy.
- *Give back to society*: Share your wealth with those who need it more than you.

The dog trainer thanks BethMari for her valuable lessons and promises to apply them in his life. He returns home with Rex and begins practicing what he has learned.

He saves part of his income every month, reduces his expenses, and invests his money in reliable businesses related to dogs, such as breeding, grooming, or selling accessories. He protects his wealth from thieves and fraudsters, learns new techniques for training dogs, prepares for unexpected events such as illness or accidents, and donates some of his money and time to help other dogs and people.

After several years of following BethMari's principles, the dog trainer becomes wealthy and respected in his town. He has many loyal customers who trust him with their dogs' training and care. He also has many friends who admire him for his generosity and kindness.

One day, he meets Dahare, who, upon hearing about the trainer's successes, challenges him to a Westminster Dog Show-style competition. Dahare boasts that he is faster and smarter than any dog or human and that he does not need input from anyone. His motto is, *"Well, if that works for you."*

The dog trainer accepts the challenge but warns Dahare that speed and confidence alone are not everything.

The competition begins, and Dahare quickly takes the lead over Rex and the trainer, who follow steadily behind him. Dahare assumes he has already won, so he decides to take a short break by a jumping obstacle to check and post on his social media.

Rex, being well-trained, seizes the opportunity and passes him without stopping.

Dahare jumps up too late and realizes that he has lost. He tries to catch up with Rex, but it is futile. Rex crosses the finish line first and wins the event.

The dog trainer celebrates with Rex and tells Dahare about the lessons he learned from BethMari—lessons he had once been unwilling to learn.

Dahare had to accept that:

- He didn't know everything.
- It was okay to admit that he didn't know.
- Slow and steady wins the race.

The trainer also tells Dahare that if he wants to be rich and happy—not just in terms of finances—he should learn from BethMari's principles instead of relying on luck, tricks, and only his own ways.

He invites Dahare to join him at his home, where he will share some of his acquired wisdom. Dahare agrees, follows him, and they become friends who learn from each other.

Slow and Steady

Our personal story about slow and steady, learning, and adapting might not be as intriguing or interesting to everyone. However, we hope it will be encouraging and inspiring to some. To illustrate this, we turn to Andrew Carnegie, as we did some reading about him.

When looking at a slow and steady approach in both dog training and financial management, we will consider a bit of Carnegie's story along with that of BethMari, the rich lady from Brush.

Andrew Carnegie's rise from humble beginnings to becoming one of the wealthiest men in history was not the result of a get-rich-quick scheme. He started working at a young age, learning the ropes of the textile industry before transitioning to the steel industry.

He was diligent, hardworking, and focused on the long-term. He reinvested his profits into his businesses and diversified his holdings. His slow and steady approach paid off in the end, allowing him to amass a fortune that enabled him to become one of the most generous philanthropists of all time.

Similarly, the trainer in the story of Rex and BethMari learned and adapted to the principle that slow and steady wins the race when it comes to building wealth through sound financial management.

- They were not impulsive.
- They did not seek instant gratification.
- They saved a portion of their income and invested it wisely, always thinking long-term.
- They were not swayed by the latest fads or trends but stuck to sound financial principles that had stood the test of time.

The Power of Consistency in Training and Finance

As dog owners, we often see people who want quick fixes for their dog's behavior problems or challenges.

44

- They may try the latest training gadget or enroll their dog in a short training program for a brief period.
- However, these quick fixes rarely produce lasting results.
- It is only through consistent training and reinforcement that a dog's behavior can be modified over the long term.

The same principle applies to personal finance.

- It's tempting to chase the latest hot stock tip or investment strategy that promises quick returns.
- However, these strategies are often risky and unsustainable.

Instead, focus on:

- Building a diversified portfolio of low-cost index funds and holding them for the long term.
- Allowing the power of compounding to work in your favor.
- Watching your wealth grow steadily over time.

Discipline in Budgeting and Investing

Another aspect of slow and steady is the importance of sticking to a budget.

- Just like a dog needs consistent reinforcement to learn good behavior, your finances need consistent attention to stay on track.
- By setting a budget and sticking to it, you can avoid impulse purchases and overspending.
- This will free up more money to invest in your future and build long-term wealth.

This is not to sound repetitive but rather to reinforce the idea that slow and steady wins the race.

It takes learning and adapting when it comes to:

- Taking care of a puppy.
- Managing personal finances effectively.

By adopting a patient and consistent approach to personal finance, you can achieve financial security and freedom.

Andrew Carnegie's life and BethMari's teachings remind us that building wealth is not a sprint but a marathon.

Just like training a dog, it takes time and effort, but the rewards are worth the effort.

The Value of Adaptation

One of Sadie's greatest lessons was the value of adaptation.

Whether it was:

- Learning to hunt mice.
- Dealing with an illness.

She taught us that flexibility is crucial.

In personal finance, life rarely goes as planned, and adapting to change—whether an unexpected expense or a market downturn—is essential.

For example:

- When Sadie fell ill, we adjusted her care routine.
- Just as we adjust our budget when faced with unexpected expenses.

Financial resilience is about creating room for the unexpected while staying focused on your goals.

Adaptation isn't about abandoning plans—it's about evolving them.

Takeaway

Be prepared to adapt. Flexibility allows you to navigate life's joys and challenges, whether caring for a beloved pet or managing your finances.

Aspect	Description
Definition	Being open to change and adjusting to new situations.
Importance	Essential for navigating life's joys and challenges.
Examples	Caring for a pet, managing finances.

Responsibility

" The leash, like a budget, keeps everything under control and prevents chaos. "

Responsibility is the duty or obligation to satisfactorily perform or complete a task that one must fulfill and which has consequences if failed. It involves accountability, reliability, and the willingness to own the outcomes of one's actions.

Taking responsibility for Sadie meant recognizing that her needs would sometimes come before our convenience. Whether it was taking her out late at night or cleaning up after her, we learned the importance of accountability. Financial responsibility works the same way. It requires owning your decisions, from creating a budget to addressing debt. Just as Sadie relied on us, your financial health depends on your ability to take consistent, reliable actions.

48

Lily and Pip

Lily, the dog trainer and owner, did not like the crate, and she did not like the leash. The leash, that metaphorical budget, felt like a cruel joke sometimes. Pip, a whirlwind of fur and puppy-dog eyes, would strain against it, his whole body a symphony of wiggles.

"Heel, Pip!" Lily would command. When she wasn't feeling bad about having Pip on a leash, she smiled nervously, her voice firm but wavering.

He'd respond with a soulful look, as if to say, *"But the squirrel! The squirrel is clearly more important than this arbitrary human construct of 'heel.'"*

It was like trying to stick to a budget while surrounded by the siren song of tempting sales and irresistible impulse buys.

She had many ups and downs with Pip. She would try to potty train him, and he would go inside. He would bark and whine incessantly until he was let out of the apartment. Then he would play, come back inside, and go again—wherever he felt like it.

He was lovable but, at times, seemed out of control.

Such were the travails of Pip.

She thought about these things as she repeatedly said, *"Sit, Pip!"* her patience wearing thinner than a pair of cheap socks.

He'd sit, of course, but only for a fleeting moment before launching himself into another chaotic exploration of the neighborhood.

It was like watching her meticulously planned savings evaporate in a single, ill-advised online shopping spree.

One day, while attempting to teach Pip the joys of *"leave it"* (a crucial skill, much like resisting the allure of that *"too good to be true"* investment opportunity), she accidentally dropped a particularly juicy treat.

Pip, with the speed of a seasoned stock market trader, snatched it up in a flash.

She felt a pang of guilt, like a careless investor who'd lost a significant portion of their portfolio.

But just like a good personal financial manager, she learned from her mistakes.

She started carrying treats in her pocket, rewarding desired behaviors with enthusiastic praise and a tasty morsel.

It was like investing in the stock market—patience, discipline, and a long-term perspective were key.

Lily knew that neglecting Pip's exercise was like neglecting her own health.

Just as a balanced diet and regular exercise were crucial for her well-being, consistent training and playtime were vital for Pip's physical and mental health.

"Sit, Pip!" she repeated, gently guiding him into the desired position.

Every day was a new lesson.

Lily learned to be patient, just as responsible investors learn to be patient with their portfolios.

She observed Pip's behavior, analyzing his reactions and adjusting her approach accordingly.

This *"curiosity"* and willingness to learn were essential in both dog training and financial management.

Pip, with his boundless energy, could easily get carried away.

- He'd chase squirrels.
- He'd bark at strangers.
- He'd jump on people.
- Sometimes, he'd even try to steal treats from the counter.

Lily, like a responsible investor, had to ensure Pip's actions had a positive impact.

She redirected his energy toward positive behaviors, rewarding good behavior and gently correcting unwanted ones.

This was like ensuring her investments aligned with her values—making sure her money contributed to a better world.

And then there were the days when she just wanted to curl up on the couch and binge-watch her favorite shows.

"Training can wait," she would rationalize. *"I deserve a break. I have enough of my own stuff to worry about."*

But just like neglecting her financial responsibilities, neglecting Pip's training had consequences.

He'd become increasingly unruly, his "budget" of acceptable behavior expanding with each passing day.

Training Pip, much like managing finances, was a constant learning experience.

It was a journey filled with laughter, frustration, and the occasional feeling of utter defeat.

But through it all, she learned the importance of patience, discipline, and the long-term rewards of responsible behavior.

And sometimes, when Pip would finally "get it"—sit, stay, leave it— she felt a sense of accomplishment that rivaled the thrill of a successful investment.

Overall, there seemed to be little bits of progress amid a sense of lack of accountability and responsibility in the ups and downs between Lily and Pip.

Although Lily had some information to get going in the right direction, Pip always looked at her in a very confused manner.

He would look at her and think, *"Where is Pip? Who is Pip? I am Walter Jackson Hayes."*

What is My Duty?

In the context of managing a puppy and finances, responsibility means acknowledging the duty to care for your pet and to manage your money wisely. This involves ensuring your puppy's health and well-being by providing proper food, shelter, medical care, and attention, much like managing finances requires budgeting, saving, and making informed financial decisions to secure your financial future. There was a time when the dog trainer saw the responsibility of taking care of a dog in a way that we did not. When we got Sadie, we each saw responsibility at different levels—from something to take care of to a fun companion that could not play fetch.

Beyond these specific tasks, whether we like it or not, we have a broader responsibility to our family and pets. Our actions and decisions directly affect their lives and well-being. We are responsible for providing a nurturing and supportive environment at home, ensuring our family members feel loved and cared for. Similarly, our pets rely on us for their happiness and survival. Thus, taking responsibility entails not only fulfilling the tasks at hand but also making sure that the needs of those who depend on us, both humans and animals, are adequately met.

One of the key areas in being responsible for a pup and finances is communication.

There is a learning process in communicating with a pup, yourself, and others in regard to money.

It is easy to talk about communication, but it is important to consider a person's agreeable mindset, morality, ethics, pride, and environment. All of those things impact how "I" think about financial matters on an individual basis and complicate interactions when dealing with others. This is a thought about communication in regard to relationships and relating with other people. We propose that the complications are not a problem with communication itself, as in being able to speak and understand what words mean, per se, but with translation. We don't have the proper translators or thesauruses to effectively express the meaning, language, words, and ideas in our heads to others in an effective manner—including both people and puppies.

For instance, we hear and read in French, while the other person hears and reads in Thai. We don't understand why the other person can't see it the way we do or why what we say is so hard to comprehend, and the reverse is also true. So we shake our heads, thinking, *"You are so hard of hearing,"* or, *"Why can't you understand? It's so simple!"* And then we have a breakdown—all the while still *"communicating."*

We connect with each other through cultural, emotional, and linguistic factors. Sometimes, we struggle to communicate because we're also thinking and feeling. Similarly, when humans communicate with dogs, there's a distinct challenge in bridging the gap between human language and canine understanding, relying more on non-verbal cues and actions.

When it comes to humans and money, communication takes on a unique dimension as people navigate financial transactions and economic relationships, where the language of currency, investments, and financial decisions can sometimes lead to misunderstandings and conflicts. In essence, effective communication is pivotal in all these interactions, whether with humans, dogs, or the world of finances.

Why all this talk about communication? Because it impacts our ability to be responsible. We can't convey responsibility without it.

With Sadie, we had to make sure we were saying the same things.

We developed hand signals. This worked when walking—a finger point meant "walk in the given direction," a closed fist meant "stop," and "with me" meant "walk beside me."

She had a blanket, a specific pink blanket, and she did not get on the couch until her pink blanket was laid on it. She also had her room, and while she did not bark a lot, she would shake her tag when she needed to go out.

One time, Sadie had gone to her spot but kept coming back to the bedroom door and shaking her tag. She ran downstairs, but not to the back door, which she would do when she needed to go outside. Instead, she stopped at the kitchen and kept looking inside. Lo and behold, there was a pot smoking on the stove. She was weirdly responsible and found a way to communicate.
Thank you Sadie!

According to P.T. Barnum, here are some responsibilities we should assume:

Responsibility to Our Health

"The foundation of success in life is good health: that is the substratum of fortune; it is also the basis of happiness. A person cannot accumulate a fortune very well when he is sick."

Barnum recognized that good health is essential for success in life, including financial success. Taking care of our health can save us money in the long run and help us achieve our financial goals.

Responsibility to Learn and Be Curious

"More persons, on the whole, are humbugged by believing in nothing than by believing too much."
Recognize the importance of being skeptical and cautious with our money. It's important to do our research and not be swayed by get-rich-quick schemes or promises that seem too good to be true.

Responsibility to Do Good and Ensure Your Money Does Good

"Money is power, and in that government which pays all the public officers of the states, all political power will be substantially concentrated."

Barnum understood the power that money can have in politics and society. It's important to be aware of how money is being used and who is controlling it in order to make informed decisions and take action when necessary.

More Actions of Responsibility:

- Creating a budget
- Tracking expenses
- Taking accountability for financial decisions
- Repeat and do it again (More Action and Responsibility)

In terms of dog behavior, some dogs exhibit aggressive or destructive tendencies, which can be dangerous and problematic for their owners and others around them.

It's important to note that a dog's behavior is largely influenced by its environment, upbringing, and training. A dog that has been mistreated, neglected, or trained poorly may exhibit bad behavior, but with proper care and training, most dogs can learn to behave appropriately and live harmoniously with their owners and others.

It's also important to remember that a dog's behavior can be complex and is not always predictable. It's up to the dog's owner to take responsibility for their dog's behavior and take steps to address any negative tendencies to ensure the safety of everyone involved. In some cases, working with a professional dog trainer or animal behaviorist may be necessary to correct problematic behavior.

Managing money is similar to taking care of pets because it requires consistent attention, discipline, and patience to ensure financial stability and growth—just as it requires the same qualities to ensure the health and well-being of pets.

Training a puppy, like managing finances, requires patience, discipline, and a long-term perspective. Responsibility involves caring for a pet's health and well-being, similar to managing finances wisely for a secure future. Beyond specific tasks, there is a broader responsibility to family and pets, ensuring their needs are met.

Effective communication is crucial for financial responsibility, as it bridges gaps between individuals, cultures, and even species.

Developing clear communication methods and consistent routines can help convey responsibility and ensure understanding. Taking responsibility for one's health, financial literacy, and the impact of money on society are also essential aspects of financial responsibility.

Responsibility means being accountable for your actions and their consequences. It includes setting boundaries. For Sadie, it meant setting boundaries—establishing where she could go, what she could do, and how we cared for her.

In personal finance, responsibility and boundaries are equally critical. Without them, spending can spiral out of control, and financial goals can be compromised.

For example, when Sadie learned to go to her designated area (*her spot*), it wasn't about limiting her freedom but ensuring her health and safety. Similarly, setting a budget and saying no to yourself and others is not about deprivation—it is about creating structure to achieve financial security. Boundaries provide the discipline required to meet responsibilities and avoid unnecessary risks.

Takeaway

Boundaries aren't restrictions; they're tools for growth and security. Set clear limits on pet ownership and financial management to ensure responsible long-term well-being. Effective communication of these boundaries allows for a sense of freedom with pets or finances.

Area	Boundary	Benefit
Pet Ownership	Set clear limits on the number and types of pets	Ensures responsible pet care and long-term well-being
Financial Management	Establish clear guidelines for spending and saving	Promotes financial security and long-term stability

Perspectives

A dog that was an obvious mix looked, to say the least, strange—it was a Shar-Pei and a Basset Hound. What stood out about this dog, besides being able to clearly identify the breeds that were mixed, was the fact that it was a very well-trained and well-behaved training dog. This looked like the result of patience and perseverance.

Perspective – Understanding Beyond Agreement

"What do you think when you see a Rottweiler? A Pit Bull? A Pomeranian? A vacation commercial online or on TV? A coupon?"

From not being dog people to having Sadie, and from having debt to becoming debt-free, we began to see people, places, and things differently. If you remember, she was our "better than a Mer-'cedes' purchase."

- Her cost was lower.
- There was no depreciation.
- Although we couldn't drive her across the country, her benefit was far greater than we expected.

We had preconceived notions, just like a lot of people. You know the look when:

- You see a dog dressed like a person.
- You see a dog—some people think dogs belong outside—sitting on its owner's lap.
- You see someone with a new car every six months, and the feeling is that they will always have a car payment.

Looking back over all the notes and scenarios from over the years, we can see that our perspective on dogs and money has changed from when we first started.

Most people have an idea or definition of perspective. Many times, it is confused with prerogative.

For the purpose of this book and the content being discussed, we will establish a common definition.

What is Perspective?

Perspective is the lens through which we interpret and make sense of the world.

It is the basis for how we and others "see" things. It also shapes how we approach:
- Challenges.
- Relationships.
- Practical matters, like managing finances or training a pet.

While our experiences, values, and cultural background influence our perspective, it's important to recognize that different perspectives exist—and that understanding them is not the same as agreeing with them.

This was briefly touched on earlier with communication, but too often, we equate understanding with agreement.

We say, *"You don't understand me,"* when what we really mean is, *"You don't agree with me."*

This is a flawed view of understanding.

A better application of understanding isn't about alignment with our own views—it's about recognizing and processing different viewpoints, even if we don't adopt them ourselves.

Understanding is like comprehending or making sense of something based on knowledge and experience—a shared understanding between people or about things.

"My dog or money don't understand me."

That might sound like a ridiculous statement, but in personal finance and dog ownership, misunderstandings often arise from failing to distinguish these definitions and differences.

"People say money is all I talk about, but when I see money, money wants to talk it out."

— Bruce Babbi

How Perspective Shapes Our Views on Dogs and Money

When we started, we pointed out that our perspective on dogs is influenced by personal experiences, culture, and upbringing. Some people see dogs as beloved family members, while others view them as working animals, status symbols, or even nuisances. Similarly, financial perspectives vary—some see money as a tool, others as a source of stress, and some as a measure of success.

Different Perspectives on Dogs:

1. **A Family Member** – People who treat their dogs as part of the family often invest heavily in their care, providing premium food, medical treatment, and even birthday parties.
2. **A Working Tool** – Farmers, police officers, and service-dog trainers may see dogs as workers, bred and trained for a specific purpose rather than as household pets.
3. **A Status Symbol** – Some people acquire expensive or rare breeds as a display of wealth and prestige.
4. **A Nuisance** – Those who have had bad experiences with dogs (such as being bitten or dealing with constant barking) may see them as a problem rather than a companion.

We came to the understanding that no single perspective is universally "right" or "wrong." The key is recognizing that different people have different experiences with dogs, which shapes how they treat and interact with them.

Different Perspectives on Money:

1. **A Tool for Freedom** – Some people view money as a means to an end—financial stability allows them to live life on their terms.
2. **A Source of Stress** – For others, money represents anxiety, debt, and struggle.
3. **A Symbol of Success** – Some equate financial wealth with self-worth or personal achievement.
4. **Something to Be Feared or Avoided** – Those who have seen financial failure or corruption may avoid engaging deeply with financial planning.

Just as with dogs, no single financial perspective applies to everyone. Recognizing that others may see money differently can improve financial discussions and decision-making.

Interestingly, these perspectives could be our own or the perspectives of other people. What do we think when we see someone with an Afghan or Portuguese Water Dog driving a Bentley, yachting, flying on a G5, or wearing a Patek Philippe watch? These are just examples—it could be a trip we saw posted on social media. Many of these things put us in a *"Wow, that person has money"* mindset.

This also impacts how we view ourselves if we don't match some of the items or activities we see from others. That is why we also look at understanding. All of the other items in this book bring us to this point—how we see ourselves, how we see others, and how we recognize similarities between dog training and personal finance.

Now that your perspective has been influenced by different understandings of expenses, budgets, and puppies, you encounter the perspectives of others.

- You start to see a car as a willingness or unwillingness to take on debt, rather than as a status symbol.
- You see a dog as a valuable companion for anyone who has one, rather than just a chore.
- You see a purse as something that holds your belongings, rather than something that signals a status you may or may not have attained.

If you own any of those things, your understanding of why and how you acquired them came from a different place than it may have before.

A Thought Exercise on Perspective

Condition: *Having a nice thing does not mean that a person has a lot of money. But if you have a million-dollar net worth, does it matter if you drive a Toyota?*
Outside of entertainers, celebrities, and high-net-worth individuals in fashion, how do we identify people with money?

What is the car most commonly driven by millionaires?

According to surveys and research from Thomas J. Stanley and Dave Ramsey, the list is dominated by Toyota and Honda.

Another challenging notion is that once you're out of debt, you should be free to spend on any luxuries or discretionary lifestyle items, right?

Not exactly.

The biggest benefit of being out of debt and having a budget is similar to having a trained dog—while you will still have some management to perform, you will have a much better-managed situation.

The Conclusion of This Thought Exercise

Imagine meeting two people.

- One is dressed in fancy clothes, wearing all the name brands you find aspirational, with expensive jewelry on their neck, wrist, and fingers.
- The other appears poor, wearing tattered clothes, cut-off shorts with a few holes.

If you are quick to praise the one in fancy clothes and give them the best place, while ignoring the one in tattered clothes, it would be an indicator that your perspective on wealth may not be as clear or as fair as you would like it to be.

You could be judging someone based on their perceived wealth, which is not only unfair but also reveals deeper motivations.

These perspectives will ultimately impact your personal financial management, dog training, and ability to control different aspects of life.

Bridging the Gap Between Perception and Understanding

Many conflicts—whether about money, relationships, or even dog ownership—stem from the belief that understanding means agreement. This false assumption creates frustration when people don't see eye to eye.

For example:
- A couple argues because one partner believes in saving aggressively, while the other enjoys spending on experiences. The spender might say, *"You don't understand me,"* when, in

reality, the saver does understand—they just have a different financial philosophy.

- A child begs for a dog, promising they'll take care of it. A parent refuses, not because they don't understand the child's excitement, but because they foresee the long-term responsibility.

In both cases, the disagreement doesn't stem from a lack of understanding but from different values and priorities.

To navigate these situations, it helps to ask:

1. *Am I assuming someone doesn't understand, or do they simply disagree with me?*
2. *Am I considering their perspective, or am I only focused on my own?*
3. *What experiences might have shaped their view, and how do they differ from mine?*

By shifting our mindset, we can communicate better and make more informed decisions—whether in finances, pet ownership, or life in general.

Application: Perspective in Action

Understanding isn't just about acknowledging differences; it's about applying that awareness in real situations.

Dog Training and Perspective:

Imagine someone who has never trained a dog before. They might think that a dog's behavior is just about personality rather than training and environment. A trainer, however, sees behavior as something that can be shaped.

Scenario:

A first-time dog owner is frustrated that their dog chews everything. They say, *"My dog is just bad."*

A trainer responds, *"I understand that it's frustrating, but chewing is normal behavior for a dog without proper outlets."*

The owner hears: *"You don't get how hard this is."*

The trainer means: *"I do get it, and that's why I'm explaining a different approach."*

The owner's frustration isn't about understanding—it's about resistance to shifting perspective. Once they reframe the situation, they can take action to correct the dog's behavior.

Personal Finance and Perspective:

Someone living paycheck to paycheck might believe that saving is impossible. A financial advisor, however, sees opportunities to adjust spending habits.

Scenario:

A person says, *"I can't save money. Every dollar is spent on necessities."*
A financial coach responds, *"I understand—it's tough. Let's break it down and see if we can find small areas to adjust."*

The person hears: *"You don't get my situation."*

The coach means: *"I do get it, and I want to help you find a different way to look at it."*

By shifting perspective, financial growth becomes possible—just like with dog training, where small adjustments lead to long-term change.

Final Thought: Adjusting Your Perspective for Growth

Whether we're talking about managing money or training a pet, perspective shapes our approach. The key takeaway is this:

- Understanding doesn't require agreement.
- People can see the same situation differently without either being "wrong."
- A shift in perspective can lead to better financial decisions, improved relationships, and stronger communication.

In both finances and pet training, growth comes when we step outside our viewpoint and consider others'. When we move beyond *"You don't understand me"* to *"Let me see that perspective,"* we create room for learning, change, and success.

Sadie taught us to view dogs and money differently, avoiding judgment based on incomplete information. Instead, she taught us to create space for learning, growth, and success.

We went from non-pet owners to pet owners, to dog owners, to dog owners looking forward to taking their dogs out on new experiences, and dog owners running home to see their dogs.

Along the way, there were misunderstandings about what to do and how to do it. We encountered different perspectives that helped move everything along.

- Could she sleep on the bed? No.
- But after some training, we were comfortable with her sleeping in one of her beds in different rooms.
- Eventually, she preferred to sleep in her room.

At a certain time of the evening, she would scratch the door of whichever room she was in, check the house to make sure everyone was where they should be, open the door to her crate, go in, and lay down.

We can admit our money is not as well trained as Sadie, but we and it are learning.

Takeaway

Perspective, shaped by experiences and values, influences how we see the world—including dogs and money.

- Different perspectives exist and are not universally right or wrong.
- Understanding different perspectives, even without agreeing with them, is crucial for effective communication and decision-making in personal finance and dog ownership.

Our perspectives on wealth, expenses, and even dog ownership are shaped by our experiences and values. We often make assumptions about others based on their outward appearance or possessions, but true understanding comes from considering their experiences and perspectives.

By shifting our mindset and embracing different viewpoints, we can improve our financial decisions, relationships, and communication skills.

Growth comes from understanding other perspectives, which leads to understanding and tools that help in training the "bad" behavior out of dog training and personal finance.

This can lead to teaching a dog new tricks, like:
- *Looking for traffic when on a walk.*
- *Coming when called.*
- *Training your money to pay off bills on time, give, save, or invest on your commands.*

Conclusion

Training a dog and managing money share a surprising truth: both require patience, discipline, and the right mindset. Whether you're raising a pet or building wealth, the key is commitment. Master these lessons, and you'll find financial freedom—without the bad habits of an untrained dog.

Most wealthy people, as defined by net worth rather than being uber-rich or celebrities, don't *feel* rich, just as most dog owners don't think their dogs are ready for the AKC National or Westminster Dog Show. However, they do recognize the rewarding and challenging experience that comes with both dogs and finances.

Some people don't like the word challenge or hard because they associate negative feelings or emotions with those words. As a result, they avoid the challenge and miss out on the rewards that come with it.

Back to the Beginning

We might have mentioned that we got Sadie from a farm—it was a five to six-hour trip. We felt like we were in strange lands and almost turned around to go home empty-handed.

At the last minute, we decided to continue down a dirt road, and at the end of the road—voilà!

We know that people have traveled much farther, at a much higher cost, to get their prized pups.

We had heard about puppy mills, as they were all over the news. With all the research we had done in looking for a dog, we were glad that the family at this farm had bred a puppy that met our requirements.

We were a tiny bit emotional and a bit saddened that we would be taking this pup away from the spacious farm. The breeder confidently told us, *"She will forget about it."*

This reminded us of a time years ago when a nicely groomed dog jumped into our van and was content with us taking it away.

We looked for a collar and a tag but did not see anything apparent.

As part of this story, it made us think:

> *"Tag your dog and tag your money; otherwise, someone will run off with it."*

Everything we have discussed in this book—notes, scenarios, and experiences—boils down to that statement and the tools used to build a decent relationship with a living animal and to have a proper relationship with an amoral thing (money) and everything it represents.

Instead of focusing on "bad" attributes, it's more helpful to consider undesirable behaviors that can pose challenges for both dogs and their owners.

Undesirable dog behaviors often stem from:

- Lack of training and socialization
- Underlying health issues
- Boredom
- Improper handling
- Breed predispositions

Dogs, Money, and the "Dog Eat Dog" Phenomenon

While writing this book, we stumbled upon some news stories about dogs and money.

You may have heard about the "dog eat dog" phenomenon, where dogs have been involved in various money-related incidents.

- *A 7-year-old Goldendoodle named Cecil ate $4,000! They had $4,000 in cash to pay for a fence, and Cecil gobbled it all up.*
- *From CNBC, we learned about Champ, a Beagle who ate $250 from an envelope.*
- *A CNN news article detailed how two stray dogs caused $350,000 in damage at a car dealership.*

These stories weren't just funny or shocking—they also highlighted how dogs can cause real financial losses.

It's just like when we make personal financial decisions that don't go as planned.

Sometimes, dogs act out because they're not properly trained or socialized. They may have underlying health issues, be bored, or be handled improperly. And some breeds are just more prone to certain behaviors.

If Dogs Aren't 'Bad,' Then Money Isn't Either

If dogs aren't *bad*, then money in our lives can be managed just like the undesirable behaviors dogs exhibit.

We identified some behaviors, and while there may be more, here are 10 undesirable behaviors that can be misinterpreted as 'bad' but actually require understanding and intervention:

10 Undesirable Dog Behaviors & Their Causes

1. *Excessive barking* – Can be caused by boredom, anxiety, separation, or territoriality.
2. *Biting* – May be playful, fear-based, or due to resource guarding (food aggression).
3. *Jumping* – Often a greeting behavior but can be overwhelming or dangerous.
4. *Destructive chewing* – Indicates boredom, anxiety, or lack of stimulation.
5. *Digging* – A natural instinct, but it can be destructive if not directed to appropriate areas.
6. *Pulling on the leash* – An untrained behavior that can be frustrating for both dog and owner.
7. *Separation anxiety* – Can manifest in destructive behaviors when left alone.
8. *Fearfulness* – May be due to past trauma or lack of socialization.
9. *Reactivity* – Aggressive or defensive behavior toward other dogs or people.
10. *Housetraining issues* – Can be due to medical problems, stress, or improper training.

Remember, every dog deserves a chance to learn and thrive.

By understanding the root causes of their behaviors, seeking professional help when necessary, and implementing positive training methods, we can transform any challenging situation into a positive one.

It's crucial to refrain from labeling dogs as inherently "bad" and instead focus on understanding their behavior and addressing the root causes of any undesirable actions.

Metaphors for Financial Management

At first glance, these 10 undesirable dog behaviors may seem unrelated to money, but they can be used as metaphors for poor financial management.

We hope you see this as a creative and insightful way to highlight the negative consequences of certain financial choices.

How Each Dog Behavior Relates to Money:

1. *Excessive Barking* – Impulse spending, wasting money on unnecessary purchases, neglecting bills.
2. *Biting* – Taking on too much debt, exceeding credit limits, making investments without proper research.
3. *Jumping* – Chasing quick wins in the market, investing in risky ventures without considering long-term goals (*Remember "Rabbit Syndrome"*).
4. *Destructive Chewing* – Neglecting savings, living paycheck to paycheck, eroding financial security.
5. *Digging* – Ignoring financial problems, burying debt instead of addressing it, avoiding budgeting and planning.
6. *Pulling on the Leash* – Lack of financial discipline, giving in to temptations, struggling to control spending habits.
7. *Separation Anxiety* – Fearing financial loss, clinging to possessions, over-reliance on a single income source.
8. *Fearfulness* – Avoiding financial decisions, paralyzed by uncertainty, neglecting investment opportunities.
9. *Reactivity* – Overreacting to market fluctuations, making impulsive decisions based on emotions like fear or greed.
10. *Housetraining Issues* – Inconsistent budgeting, neglecting financial hygiene, lack of accountability in managing finances.

By using these metaphors, it becomes easier to understand the negative impact of certain financial behaviors.

Just as undesirable dog behaviors can be corrected through training and positive reinforcement, bad financial habits can be corrected through education, planning, and responsible financial practices.

Final Thought: Train Your Money Like a Well-Behaved Dog

Similar to how we wouldn't label a dog as *bad* for its behavior, it's important to approach financial challenges with understanding and a willingness to learn.

By identifying and addressing these financial *"barking"* and *"biting"* behaviors, we can work toward a more secure and stable financial future.

We hope this creative interpretation provides a new perspective on financial management!

A Sobering Reality About Dogs & Financial Management

According to one study, the average age of dogs that enter shelters is 18 months, and their owners relinquish 26.3% of shelter intakes.

If greater financial management meant fewer puppies in shelters, imagine the impact.

Perhaps those who train their money can also afford to adopt and train a dog.

Managing money is much like training a dog. Both require patience, consistency, and adaptability. Through our experiences with Sadie, we discovered that small, deliberate actions—whether setting a budget or teaching a dog to sit—can lead to meaningful outcomes.

As you take the lessons from this book into your own life, remember:
- Discipline and responsibility are not constraints; they are foundations of freedom and success.

Epilogue

On April 11, 2023, Sadie passed away.

The night before, everything seemed fine—until it wasn't. She had run up and down the stairs and grabbed her snack earlier in the day. Then, in the evening, she just laid down.

We already had a vet appointment scheduled for the next day because we thought she had an unrelated issue, so we just figured that once we got her to the vet, everything would be fine.

That night, she went up the stairs but did not go to her room, which raised concerns. However, she eventually went to her room and laid down.

In the morning, she said *good morning* in the way she normally did. Then, approximately two hours later, she was discovered to have passed.

We took her to the vet, and this information was confirmed.

Yes—it was sad.

Before she passed, we had been thinking about getting another puppy so that Sadie could train the new dog in the same way that she had been trained.

She was an old dog interested in new tricks, and it would have been fun to see her whip a new puppy into shape because she was a Lady!

In any event, it took some time to adjust to not having her watch the house and watch over us.

We concluded that maybe she had reached the end of her lessons— that she had been looking out for us in the way she knew how.

In the end, after all these years, her passing became one of the inspirations for us to finally finish this book, these notes, and everything that had been over 10 years in the making.

With Sadie, we became debt-free and got a puppy that should have been named Ramsey but was better than a Mercedes. She influenced our budget, our spending, and how we look at dogs, people who have dogs, and even those who don't have dogs. It was more than we thought we were getting. Today, Sadie is still paying for stuff, and we are still reaping the benefits—it's the discipline that was established.

In 2024, we dog-sat Kobe for a few days. Kobe was the dog-in-law of a relative. It was good therapy. We realized there were some things that we missed, some things we did not, and ultimately, dog sitting also seemed like a clincher. No other dog would be Sadie. We were so used to the way Sadie moved, sounded, and communicated. Kobe made us a little uncomfortable. We seemed a little like we did not know where he was or what he was doing. We additionally realized this is what happens with money when you don't know it. It makes us uncomfortable, and it should. Just like we became comfortable with Kobe, you can become comfortable with money.

The goal of comparing these two different things is not to make you rich but to help you become enriched with man's best friend and the other that should be man's servant.

Source Information: A Wealth of Knowledge

Because we know we are not experts in finances or dog training, we have included notes and additional information on dog training and personal financial management.

Along with this book, here are some ways you can use the personal finance advice provided to build wealth over time. Of course, many other factors can affect your wealth, such as luck, inheritance, entrepreneurship, or innovation.

In terms of chance, note:

- 13.5% of people win in the Casinos
- 1 in 300 million people win the lottery
- 70-75% of millionaires are debt free
- Richest Americans Don't Feel Wealthy
  - https://www.kiplinger.com/investing/wealth-management/richest-americans-dont-feel-wealthy

By following these basic principles, you can increase your chances of achieving financial security and independence.

We saw dog breeds as analogous to different financial situations in some regards. Some dogs require more training or different types of training, just as different people have varying financial situations. The starting point for training may differ, but the underlying principles remain the same.

Regardless of your starting point, the bulleted items below, along with this book, provide valuable information to consider when getting started or moving forward.

Personal Finance Sources

Reputable finance experts and organizations:
- *Ramsey Solutions*
- *Consumer Financial Protection Bureau*
- *Vanguard, Fidelity, etc.*

Dog Training Sources

Recognized animal behaviorists and organizations:
- *American Kennel Club*
- *Karen Pryor Academy*
- *American Veterinary Medical Association*

The Core Principles of Financial Discipline

There is no single or easy way to become wealthy, but using the personal finance advice we shared can help you improve your financial situation and achieve your goals.

Here are some possible ways to use the information to build wealth:
- Use the SMART framework to set specific, measurable, achievable, relevant, and time-bound financial goals
  - https://www.investopedia.com/managing-wealth/simple-steps-building-wcalth/
  - For example, you could set a goal to save $10,000 for a down payment on a house in two years or to retire with $1 million in 25 years
- Create a budget that allows you to live below your means and save as much as possible.
  - Use the debt avalanche method to pay off your high-interest debt first, and avoid taking on new debt unless it is necessary and beneficial
  - https://www.investopedia.com/managing-wealth/simple-steps-building-wealth/
  - https://www.forbes.com/advisor/investing/how-to-get-rich/
- Build an emergency fund of at least $1,000 and ideally three to six months of expenses, so that you can handle unexpected costs without resorting to debt or dipping into your savings
  - https://www.investopedia.com/managing-wealth/simple-steps-building-wealth/
  - https://hbr.org/2022/03/how-to-build-wealth-when-you-dont-come-from-money
  - https://hbr.org/2022/11/5-ways-to-manage-your-personal-finances
- Invest your money in a diversified portfolio of low-cost index funds and ETFs, and take advantage of tax-advantaged accounts like Roth

IRAs and 401(k) plans. Don't try to time the market or chase returns, but instead invest consistently and for the long term
- https://www.investopedia.com/managing-wealth/simple-steps-building-wealth/
- https://www.forbes.com/advisor/investing/how-to-get-rich/
- https://hbr.org/2022/11/5-ways-to-manage-your-personal-finances

- Maximize your income potential by investing in your education and skills, seeking opportunities for career advancement, and negotiating your salary and benefits
  - https://www.investopedia.com/managing-wealth/simple-steps-building-wealth/
  - https://hbr.org/2022/03/how-to-build-wealth-when-you-dont-come-from-money
  - https://www.kiplinger.com/personal-finance/steps-to-help-build-wealth
- Protect your assets by reviewing your insurance coverage regularly and ensuring you have adequate protection for your life, health, home, and car.
- Create a will and an estate plan to ensure your wealth is distributed according to your wishes
  - https://www.investopedia.com/managing-wealth/simple-steps-building-wealth/
  - https://hbr.org/2022/03/how-to-build-wealth-when-you-dont-come-from-money
  - https://hbr.org/2022/11/5-ways-to-manage-your-personal-finances
- Understand the impact of taxes on your wealth and look for ways to minimize your tax liability
- Contribute to a traditional IRA, 401(k), or other government or employer provided investment program to reduce your taxable income, or use a health savings account (HSA) to pay for medical expenses with pre-tax dollars
  - https://www.investopedia.com/managing-wealth/simple-steps-building-wealth/
  - https://hbr.org/2022/11/5-ways-to-manage-your-personal-finances
  - https://www.kiplinger.com/personal-finance/steps-to-help-build-wealth

According to leading financial experts, consistency and routine are the cornerstones of successful personal finance management. Here's a summary of best practices gathered from highly respected sources:

Income & Expenses:

- *Track consistently*: Monitor your income and expenses religiously. For apps, spreadsheets, or pen-and-paper work, choose a method that suits you and stick to it. (Sources: *Ramsey Solutions, The Finance Bar*)
- *Automate*: Set up automatic bill payments and transfers to savings/investments to avoid missed payments and ensure financial goals stay on track. (Sources: *Consumer Financial Protection Bureau, NerdWallet*)
- *Budget regularly*: Review and adjust your budget monthly or biweekly to reflect changing needs and spending habits. (Sources: *J. L. Collins, The Simple Dollar*)

Saving & Investing:

- *Pay yourself first*: Treat savings like a bill and prioritize it. Aim for 10-20% of your income, starting with 1% and gradually increasing. (Sources: *Suze Orman, Dave Ramsey*)
- *Invest consistently*: Contribute to retirement accounts and long-term investments regularly, even if it's a small amount. Time in the market matters more than timing the market. (Sources: *Vanguard, The Motley Fool*)
- *Compound interest*: Leverage the power of compounding by reinvesting dividends and earnings. Start early and watch your money grow exponentially. (Sources: *Albert Einstein, Investor.gov*)

Debt Management:

- *Prioritize high-interest debt*: Tackle credit cards and other high-interest debt first using methods like the avalanche or snowball approach. (Sources: *Mark Cuban, The National Foundation for Credit Counseling*)
- *Avoid unnecessary debt*: Be mindful of impulse purchases and unnecessary credit card usage. Pay cash if you can, have a plan and if you must, only borrow what you can comfortably afford to repay. (Sources: *The Balance, Investopedia*)
- *Develop a debt repayment plan*: Create a realistic plan to pay off debt and track your progress. Celebrate milestones to stay motivated. (Sources: *The Debt Snowball, The Penny Hoarder*)

Financial Education:
- *Continuously learn*: Read books and articles, listen to podcasts, and attend workshops to stay updated on financial concepts and strategies. (Sources: *Khan Academy, BiggerPockets*)
- *Seek professional advice*: Consult a certified financial planner for personalized guidance, especially for complex situations or significant life changes. (Sources: *The Garrett Planning Network, The National Association of Personal Financial Advisors*)
- *Stay informed*: Be aware of financial scams and frauds. Protect your personal and financial information diligently. (Sources: *Federal Trade Commission, Consumer Financial Protection Bureau*)

Remember, consistency and routine are key, but flexibility is crucial, too. Life throws curveballs, so adapt your approach while holding onto your core financial goals. By incorporating these best practices, you'll be well on your way to building a secure and prosperous economic future.

Consistency & Routine: The Golden Rules of Dog Training

When it comes to effective dog training, leading veterinary and animal behavior experts unanimously agree on the importance of consistency and routine.

Here's a summary of best practices gleaned from their insights:

Training & Cues:
- *Use one word/action per command*: Stick to a single verbal cue or gesture for each behavior (e.g., "sit" means sit, not "down" or "butt scoot"). Confusion slows learning. (Sources: *American College of Veterinary Behaviorists, Karen Pryor Academy*)
- *Be consistent in delivery*: Use the same tone, volume, and body language each time you give a command. Avoid mixing things up. (Sources: *The Association for Pet Dog Trainers, Dr. Sophia Yin*)
- *Practice daily, even for short bursts*: Brief, consistent training sessions (5-10 minutes) are more effective than occasional long

ones. (Sources: *International Association of Animal Behavior Consultants, Victoria Stilwell*)

Rewards & Corrections:
- *Reward desired behavior instantly*: Reinforce correct actions with treats, praise, or playtime within seconds of them happening. (Sources: *American Kennel Club, Patricia McConnell*)
- *Be consistent with corrections*: Never reward unwanted behavior. Address it calmly and immediately with a firm "no" or redirection. (Sources: *The Humane Society of the United States, Cesar Millan*)
- *Avoid mixed messages*: Everyone interacting with the dog should follow the same training rules and expectations. (Sources: *Institute of Certified Dog Trainers, Monks of New Skete*)

Routine & Structure:
- *Set predictable feeding & walking times*: Consistency in basic needs creates security and helps prevent unwanted behaviors. (Sources: *American Veterinary Medical Association, Dr. Ian Dunbar*)
- *Establish calming rituals*: Dedicate specific play, training, and relaxation times to build good habits and manage energy levels. (Sources: *Dr. Pamela Reid, Patricia McConnell*)
- *Practice in various environments*: Gradually expose your dog to different distractions to ensure learned behaviors generalize. (Sources: *The Association of Professional Dog Trainers, Karen Pryor Clicker Training*)

When it comes to dog training, patience and positive reinforcement are key. Celebrate small wins, manage expectations, and seek professional help if needed.

By adhering to these consistency and routine principles, you'll build a strong foundation for a happy, well-behaved, and confident canine companion.

Acknowledgements

This book would not have been possible without the love, support, and wisdom of many individuals who have contributed to our journey.

First and foremost, we thank God for blessing us with the inspiration, patience, and perseverance to bring this book to life.

To Grandma, there is a song, *"little things mean a lot...appreciate what you've got...don't sit around and wait for all the big things in your life..."* which encapsulates the words and the impact of the words. We appreciate all the little things, and they do mean a lot!

To our family and friends —you are the heart of this project. Your contributions, insights, and shared experiences have made this book what it is today. Additionally, writing this together as a family has been one of the most rewarding experiences of our lives.

To our friends, mentors, and financial coaches, including those who first introduced us to the principles of financial literacy—thank you for your guidance and encouragement. The conversations, advice, and support you've provided over the years have shaped much of what is written here. This includes a special shout out to and special thank you to Ron Blue, Larry Burkett, Dave Ramsey, and Robert Kiyosaki, whose guidance and encouragement from afar through your writings have added depth and wisdom to this book.

To Sadie, our gone but not forgotten beloved Miniature Schnauzer, who unknowingly became the best financial coach we never expected. Your antics, training, and life lessons taught us more about money and discipline than we could have imagined.

To our readers, thank you for taking the time to join us on this journey. We hope this book helps you tame your finances, build discipline, and create the financial freedom you deserve.

And finally, to everyone who believed in this project, provided feedback, or simply listened to our ideas, quirkiness, etc. —your support means the world to us.

With gratitude,
The Family

About the Authors

This book is a collaborative effort by the Bellot family—Toni, Gerald, Aaron, Anthony, Gerald III, and Jekhari are advocates for financial and business literacy. Having personally experienced life on a budget and the challenges of staying the course to financial freedom, they bring both practical wisdom and real-life insights to the table.

The Bellot family is known for engaging in deep, thought-provoking discussions where they explore a wide range of concepts about life, growth, and financial independence. Their journey is shaped by a strong commitment to learning, entrepreneurship, volunteerism, and athletics, offering them a unique perspective on success and resilience.

With diverse backgrounds and expertise, each family member contributes valuable knowledge to this book. Toni Bellot shares her personal experiences in financial planning and family management, offering practical advice on budgeting, saving, and achieving financial peace. Alongside Gerald, Aaron, and Anthony, the family has embraced financial discipline and entrepreneurial thinking from an early age—whether through running small businesses as children or navigating college expenses through scholarships and strategic money management.

Their collective experiences serve as a testament to the principles shared in this book, offering readers not just theoretical knowledge but insights for achieving financial stability and success.

Lastly, they Thank God through the ups and the downs and the lessons learned through it all.

Money is "like" a Bad Dog
Learn how to train your dog, manage your money, and build financial freedom

Is your money out of control, running wild like an untrained dog?

Managing your finances can feel overwhelming just like raising a mischievous puppy. But what if the key to financial success was as simple as training a dog?

In Money is "Like" a Bad Dog, the Bellot Family take you on a fun, engaging journey where they reveal how the principles of dog training, discipline, consistency, patience, and adaptability apply to money management.

Through humorous stories, real-life lessons, and practical financial tips, this book will teach you how to:

-Break bad money habits (like a dog breaking the habit of chewing your shoes!)

-Avoid "Rabbit Syndrome" the financial equivalent of chasing every impulse buy

-Use simple strategies to budget, save, and invest without stress

-Build financial discipline that sticks just like successful dog training

If you've ever struggled to stay on top of your finances, this book will train your money before it trains you!

A must-read for dog lovers and finance beginners alike "practical, insightful, and wildly entertaining!

Ready to tame your money? Start your financial journey today!

A must read for dog lovers and finance beginners alike "practical, insightful, and wildly entertaining